salmonpoetry

Publishing Irish & International
Poetry Since 1981

CW00404902

the arts council / an chomhairle ealaíon

funding literature

artscouncil.ie

How We Arrive
In Winter
Liz Quirke

Published in 2021 by
Salmon Poetry
Cliffs of Moher, County Clare, Ireland
Website: www.salmonpoetry.com
Email: info@salmonpoetry.com

Copyright © Liz Quirke, 2021

ISBN 978-1-912561-28-96-4

All rights reserved. No part of this publication may be reproduced or transmitted in any form or by any means, electronic or mechanical, including photography, recording, or any information storage or retrieval system, without permission in writing from the publisher. The book is sold subject to the condition that it shall not, by way of trade or otherwise, be lent, resold or otherwise circulated without the publisher's prior consent in any form of binding or cover other than that in which it is published and without a similar condition, including this condition, being imposed on the subsequent purchaser.

Cover Photograph: *"Diamond Hill" by Pearl Phelan*
Cover Design & Typesetting: *Siobhán Hutson*

Printed in Ireland by Sprint Print

Salmon Poetry gratefully acknowledges the support of
The Arts Council / An Chomhairle Ealaíon

In memory of Tom Quirke

24 November 1947 – 7 August 2018

Acknowledgements

Some of the poems appeared in the following publications: *The North, Channel, The Manchester Review, Poetry Ireland Review, Days of Clear Light - A Festschrift in Honour of Jessie Lendennie & in Celebration of Salmon Poetry at 40* (Salmon, 2021), *Impossible Archetype, Pendemic, Hold Open the Door: A Commemorative Anthology from the Ireland Chair of Poetry, Empty House: Poetry and Prose on the Climate Crisis* (Doire Press, 2021), *The Stinging Fly – The Galway 2020 Edition.*

I am grateful to the Galway Doctoral Research Fellowship at NUI Galway and to the Irish Research Council Government of Ireland Postgraduate Scholarship, the support of which was invaluable to me in the completion of this collection.

My thanks to Dr Rebecca Barr, Dr Lorna Shaughnessy, Dr Clíodhna Carney, Dr Elizabeth Tilley, Dr Adrian Paterson, Dr Charlotte McIvor, Mike McCormack and Dr John Kenny and the School of English and Creative Arts at NUI Galway for their support and for giving me a home for this creative work.

I would like to acknowledge the Irish Writers' Centre and Maria McManus for a place on the XBorders: Transitions Project.

My thanks as always to my family, friends and to Salmon Poetry.

Contents

"A prayer for the dead alive inside the living"
— Emily Berry

"Everything good and strong about me starts with my parents"
— Roxanne Gay

How We Arrive In Winter

i

We luxuriate beneath the jacaranda while it rains.
You discard all your coverings, utter a challenge
as we inhabit this, our first deluge. I keep myself
together, understand you're here with me only
because you can't be there. The water pushes
into your pores, threatens to flood you with reminders
of how confining our small courtyard
all the way across the world really is.

It rains. You scratch furrows into your skin, endure
this Sydney summer rainstorm like I've handed you
an unwelcome gift. She has been dead a month.
You mind the roadside graveyard where you left her,
all its lonely territories, so any time life blooms in unexpected
ways, you clutch it till your body racks and heaves.
We're too young in our love to have the words for this.
No one can tell me when the right thing to say will come.

ii

In this grief memory we are making, for you I can be brave.
I drop my shorts and shirt to meet yours, experience
the way the confines of this continent shatter you.
I meet you where you hold yourself aching,
settle in your wake until I am not 23 and awkward.
Eventually the rainfall slows, clothes migrate
to the open-top washer, and we endure season
after season until ten whole years pass by.

It rains on ash boughs now instead of fragrant frangipani.
We root ourselves in dark brown soil, where once
our earth loomed red. At night we see our breath,
and cold to your bones, you say, *can you believe she's dead*
so long. I say *I dreamed him the other night but he couldn't speak.*
I've forgotten his voice outside of how he said my name.
This is how we arrive in winter, how we can stand to stay
outside, breathing as all we love turns to mulch.

iii

Sometimes I wish we suspended time in that shotgun
house on Camden Street; that we had the safety
of the middle room, where we nested into each other like fledglings.
When it's bad, I ask you could we ever go back,
could we try unanswer the phonecalls that carried us home.
I see myself back at my desk, the hard yards between Newtown
and Rhodes soften — *worksleepworksleepworksleepwork*
weekday beers with Rich and Sam in the Courty.

It's then I remember times when my phone would blare and it's him,
always him calling and I describe the platforms I wait on,
how the air feels acrid and too warm in my mouth
and we talk out all news and non-news through Strathfield,
Stanmore, lose him under the bridge to Newtown, tell him
I'll call him again when I'm up on King Street, and when I do
the conversation turns to this and that, I promise him
I'm safe, I'm nearly home, I'm nearly home, I'm nearly home.

The First Forgetting

In the hours of the first forgetting, the brain
stores memories like glass shards in a palm.
I'm combing beaches kept in old photographs,
relying on muscle memory to shape my mouth
around riddles my father kept on the tip of his tongue.

Today, helicopters circle and eleven days from Christmas
I tell the children it's Santa checking
for lights, letters, to see if they have behaved –
they're too young to equate the rotor's cut
with suicide by drowning, the gloom of Galway Bay

the morning after, too new to predict a crew circling back
in pattern, how high-vis seekers line where water meets sand,
eyes skirting from rock pool to horizon and back.
Our eldest saw someone jump from the weir, we lied
in the same instant, told her the person was merely swimming,

she found it *silly he had his clothes on and*
he didn't have any goggles either. This forgetting is not
what I expected. Scenes from mornings when I crept from
the foot of the bed and everything was warm and safe and my parents
in their dawn-lit room were familiar to my senses as breathing.

The Promise of Sweetbread

i

Like everything
this begins in the tissue;
mutation concealed
where no light gathers

and it is left to me to explain
how a delicacy
can be fashioned
from such offending material,

demonstrate
how to pluck items
from your torso
to defend
and keep you longer.

Milk white,
a telling liquor
from the drain
in your side,

dislodged poison
spilling your secrets
millimetre
by marked up millilitre.

I've already promised
that I'll make something new
from this,
articulate instructions you've left
in soluble particles

to adhere to my own structures
for always,
ridged in the moss plied
from your paving stones,
ways to give new life
to listless,
unmoving articles.

ii

I'm chaperoning mementoes
             like you showed me,
corralling, deciding
             which meat meets the scrapheap
and what these days will keep.

So come beside me
             while you can argue such vanity,

help me

raze totems from their ward-wall lurking.

Split hairs with me over
      thymus *throat gullet*
verses
      pancreas *heart belly.*

We can talk immunity and t-cells
over steeping blends
from deepest darkest non-geography,
that loose leaf
that comes out on occasion,
weddings mostly,
not this time
when the priest calls to the door.

      They have email addresses on cards now,
      such a foul piece of architecture,
            worse than a lo-call number.

iii

I won't get there on time

       but parts of you
               are in my pocket.

I'll hide them in my upper anterior,
       directly behind my sternum
and I challenge
any tape measuring box ticker to crack me open.

I'm keeping your elements until
I can devise a recipe bold enough
to sweeten
with all the things you promised,

the inner body items
that require all the stars
in the system, pink grey lobes,
those splitting molecules
that recognise
that there has never been
            such a call
           for light
               as this.

While Waiting For News Of Him

I send snapshots of Galway Bay,
breakfast of fruits and grains,
rhododendron and the riverbank at college,
hold for a flower to obscure background graffiti.

I give you the best, untrue parts of my morning
and for a lack of something to say,
I try *it's raining here*, even though it is not raining,
even though we have had eleven weeks of sunshine
and not since 1976 have farmers been so put upon.

You say *it'll probably start here soon*,
even though we both know it isn't forecast,
but we've managed to pass this conversation
like a cigarette and we will let it burn quietly down
until one of us is left with scorched fingers.

While waiting for news of him,
as though sent directly from your blinking eye,
you develop an image where you sit
under a statue of St Thérèse who I mistake
for The-Blessed-and-Most-Holy-Virgin-Mary.

You call me a pagan and (how good we are at waiting)
you say *The-Blessed-and-Most-Holy-Virgin-Mary-
Always-Wears-Blue* and I say *maybe
she wanted a change*, maybe she was disgusted
by the pigment and it's peaceful associations

— wide blue yonder, blue, serenity, pure air and sky,
pious, tranquil, never-ending calm. Did she never want to scream,
poor-Most-Blessed-Mary? I consider Saint-Thérèse-
the-little-flower and her brown robe, her shelf outside the ward,
but they don't call them wards, do they?

When we wait for news of him, you there and me here,
it's always The X Unit, The Y Unit, and the saint outside
to foreshadow how bad the news will be. Thérèse and the colour
of dirt under fingernails, home and hearth and healing,
the earth we go back to again and again,

and we know while waiting for news of him
that there will be no healing here,
no glory-to-god-in-the-highest, just Thérèse
and her brown robes and our waiting.

It's Not The Work, It's The Journey
That Kills You

i

It all came to a halt the day of his accident —
    a factory-shut Saturday, machines and men on standby,
the weekday workers nursing sick heads
    over soccer fixtures, the form of horses,
except for my father

who in the brightness of that Tralee morning,
    asked if I'd keep him company on a job.

I was his eight-year-old apprentice,
    all terrible fringe and polyester tracksuit.

His talk was mechanics, pistons and crankshafts.

Back then, his body held the logic
    of a complete circuit.

He loved to quiz me.
    Name the terminals of a diode?
        Is it anode and cathode, Dad?

He gave me my own little snippers to strip flex,
    taught me to feel for when the casing gave,

how to twist my wrist just so, never slash through the wiring.
    cut only as much as is needed, be careful, he said,
    think of them as veins —
the live brown, yellow/green earthed two tone,
    single reds and blues,

oxygenated and deoxygenated.

ii

I'd wait at the gate to see him
turn into the Avenue at six,
blood blisters under his nails,
grease in the cut valleys of his hands,
all delicate strength, precise application,
always a kiss for my mother.

We would have driven that Saturday,

even though it was 300metres at most,
out the Avenue, up the Rock, left after Urban Terrace.
He would have had his tools that day —
the blue steel box from AnCO, his New York hammer,
cases of spanners, his various spools of cable,
tidy in the boot of his Granada.

iii

The musician had quoted him in the inlay of his album —

 It's not the work, it's the journey that kills you

a conversation between two Avenue boys
who took the boat at different times,
  with only one returning,

their hop-ball kept to blue-moon phone calls,
cassette sleeves, later, a signed *Roy Rogers*
on the wall of the small sitting room,

 for my friend Tom, from your friend Christie

iv

Their widows exchanged messages.

One heard weeks too late.

She sent white roses.

v

That day, when we arrived to check the roof tank,
the factory was deadbolted, all ladders locked inside.

I kicked around the delivery slipway,
airborne shrapnel rippling out into the derelict green
between St Brendan's Park and Connolly,
those spaces that terrified me at night,

how the blackness would spark
with the blaze
of contraband teenage cigarettes.

Back then, rebellion was all smoking;
drinking was for the dole queue men,

their worn denim jeans, sunken, sallow faces,
their parched mouths shaping around the same few stories
of Kilburn high road, the sites and pubs of Derby,
over weekday pints in the Pig and Whistle.

vi

I was eight, so rather than witness my father triangulate
his method of moving from one elevation to another,

I watched the Gallowsfield boys tussle over a football,
their dancing feet and sly-dig hands.

I tracked the woman who cut a quick cross along the dirt track,
hauling the usual two bags of messages from Dunnes or Barry's shop.

She could have been any of the Balloonagh girls' mothers.

vii

Dawdling in the piles of offcuts
and packaging,

I heard my name called
down from a height,

his big wave,
his castle king vantage.

Back down he scrambled,
he said *the tank is slow to fill.*

Why his job was to keep a ballcock's eye,
I'll never understand.

We'd plot the course together once more
before my child patience ran out

and I begged to stay at home.

I remember he wasn't happy
with me when he left.

viii

I can't recall the whereabouts of my mother.

Where was Maureen? Sean Óg?

The afternoon shifts

from my spot on the living room carpet

to the phone ringing,

the tearing of a noise from a throat,

an ambulance screaming across Brewery Road,

its urgency sailing up over the graveyard

and in through our open back windows.

ix

I learned later (I don't know when)
that he had shinned up one more time,

a wooden crate, corrugated iron gate,
to the flat roof and the filling tank waiting.

I wasn't there when the crate splintered away,

when the furrow of the gate tore the heart
of his wrist and sliced his palm clean.

I wasn't there when the stranger tethered his flesh
with a belt.

I never saw the signs of his pain on the slipway.

x

I learned the meaning of words like "severed,"

had trusted my sister's black biology text book

to explain the function of an "artery".

He was gone a long time.

My mother would ring from the hospital payphone.

When he came home, he covered his hand in a goatskin glove.

For years, he couldn't drive, or write, or hold a knife.

I was afraid of the tender rawness,

the lifeless buckle of his third and fourth fingers.

Items Can Be Purchased Separately

i

Category: Coffin Interior
OCEAN TWEED

A quilted interior with dark
ocean blues
and golden toned tweed design.

It features:

a golden sandstone ruffled surround,
quilt and soft comforting mattress
with tweed design pillow.

ii

Category: Casket Range
THE BOG OAK CASKET

An exceptional full lid casket
made from knotty oak
with many light and dark tones.

It features:

A hand waxed finish
with handles
and a premium
quality interior.

I try to remember him

in the kitchen; I project this attempt onto a silver screen imagined
between the presses — to reclaim recollection by max-volume-ing
                                                          Willie Nelson

so somehow we're *on the road again* with *Georgia on our minds*, back *minding
the bellies* at the apex of the humpback bridge driving towards Ardfert.
This version of him is smiling in the top-left corner of a photo with
                                                      all the aul stock,

1990s TQ, Head & Shoulders clean hair and his light beige jacket,
behind Nana Kit, Mrs Door, the Avenue women, names I won't
                                                commit to this paper,

they're all there, woven tight as a family behind Fr Broderick;
        two heads from the other branch slotted beside Fr Horgan
and whatever perpetual trophy he's brandishing towards the lens,

but those were different days, all woollen jumpers and Church-bell Sundays,
regular devotions and gate-post chat, cups of tea out over the back wall
                                                              while Dad
frittered Spring mornings with Sean two doors down.

        I'll keep these garden shed fellas with me, hold their engine oil palms
in my hands, recall the layouts of their rose bordered gardens,
as clear as the nails and Rawlplugs TQ kept in his "outside jacket" pockets,
                                                    stray bolts and screws

that *might come in handy* between coins, his important bits and pieces —
the touch of smooth metal as familiar as walking up the Rock
                                                  by Billy Naughton's

after a round of the Green and a tour of quiet curving streets down by Pres
and the shop where my brother bought that Honda 50. Back in the now where
                                                          much is lost,

the song changes to *always on my mind* and the scene cuts to the back
seat of the Granada again on every Sunday drive, no shatterings, no losings.
I'm three days off thirty-four, not nearly hungover after festivities

and subdued fireworks down the road with the Keogh Mullens
and this morning requires every noise-making appliance at full tilt
                                                          so nothing
settles while the spin-cycle churns through hysterics with only short
                                                    gasps between.

Going To Ground

        hope he's holed up in an archive of weekend melodies
memories of how after breakfast they would dance
        been advised to dig, keep sinking a spade till I hit hell
or acceptance, but this is beyond me, a mirage of the fires that stole
        my sleep when lullabies were my parents' low voices
lifting up through the floorboards. My dreams now see him dead
        and he offers his armchair to soothe my rattling bones
he knows I've never spoken about being alone in the house
        after leaving the hospital the first time. I used my old key
slipped through, spectral behind his cars, fired up the Landrover
        and frightened poor Brigitta across the road
How I didn't know we would rely on the aul stock
        Sonya and her mother and their bags of tea and biscuits
the way I was quick to introduce my wife, even though
        it has been decades since we spent evenings playing kerbs
They're all gone now, the big strong men of the Avenue
        Sonya's grandad, my father, those who knew each other
since short pants, handball alleys — when getting a job was more likely
        than anything and if you had a trade to your name
and your own box of tools, you were made

Words For After

When asked how he died, this is all I'll say,
it was on the day before the travels, after all their bags were packed.
A sudden death, fifteenth of June, lunchtime on a Thursday.

I'll tell them all how quick it was, one sharp pain and *that's the way*,
(we heard the phone ringing, but he never called the office back)
when asked how he died, this is all I'll say,

I'm writing out the ambulances, how we thundered night to day,
chasing blue lights over county lines, I'll clear this from the facts,
leave him a sudden passing, fifteenth of June, lunchtime on a Thursday.

I'm cutting out the rushed goodbyes, whispers to stoop and pray,
I'll split the scene and never spill the parts that I can't hack.
When asked how he died, this is all I'll say,

some days (when I can) I'll simply nod and walk away,
I won't relive the ending in retellings back to back,
his sudden death, fifteenth of June, at lunchtime on a Thursday.

I'm giving him an out more kind than the actual run of play,
no Lee view room, no God is Good, no terminal decay.
When asked when he died, this is what I'll say, it was:
an easy death, fifteenth of June, at lunchtime on a Thursday.

Vaya Con Dios

for Mikey

"'Vaya con Dios,' she said. But Clare knew now, as she had not
four years ago, that this is what the Spaniards say."

— Kate O'Brien, *As Music and Splendour*

A Thursday between here and after, we venture towards a session
in Spanish Point. My father, your grandfather, suspended ill,
isn't anywhere, isn't even dead, so in his name tonight,
I put miles between my car and Killimer's ferry dock,
grasp the invite to join you and the kind-eyed boys
and we chase cold pints and assembly along Clare's tattered coast.

This "second-summer" you've set your anchor to drag the river
where I send all my words to swim. At Ennistymon,
on the banks of the Inagh, we begin, my sister's second son and I,
to churn up such mischief as will bridge the decade I've waited for
    this company.
Composed, all six-foot-plus, at the back of Salmon's weekday theatre,
you wait, bear respectful witness to the friendships a poetic life can forge.

After, we thaw in Lahinch's Shamrock, grow warmer still at The Nineteeth.
You translate what you know of your prodigal aunt into who you see
    in this bar.
And I understand I can't boast traction in the story from your hand,
know little beyond your babyhood and snippets doled out across
    the distance,
but as Duarte saw the soul-sure "split" in Kate O'Brien's Clare,
for years I've seen how heart-stark scrutiny can fail to tether a body.

You tell me you have come of age alongside rivers,
Lee, Shannon, Llobregat, Besòs and onwards now to the Inagh,
and brave in this late hour, you ease towards memories of my own,
how I knew when I told how it all transpired who said what and when
I arm you with keepsakes from my travels, souvenirs of leaving and returning,
show you, nephew, that our lives don't have to look so different from the rest.

At The Armada, Willie Clancy is in his afters and a bouncer caught by a
    light-quick trick
sends me to dive, delighted, deep into the swell of my purse. I surface, haul
a squall-torn license, confront a likeness from my tough days of being
    asked and telling
and then all around us is carnival as the singers blast out *The Rose of Tralee*.
We reel and jig through talk of your grandfather, my father,
    make promises that we
will have more nights like this, safe from all that is approaching us in the dark.

At The Funeral Home

Cut to an ebony dais; the five of us blocked as points on a compass
in our newly ordained order.

Beside the undertaker [with folder, pen, pressed shirt, comfortable noose/
matching tie, the very fine cut of gentleman] we rank as follows:

Sister1-Mother-Me-Brother-Sister2- until back to the undertaker once more.
I will certainly eyeball this rotation time and again and again and time

throughout this awful fact-establishing coffin-selecting inquisition.
We inhabit the clothes we wore when without warning nine hours ago

my father took it upon himself to die.

I'm listen-watching this conversation do the rounds while tracing pink flowers
at the end of my sleeve, my index finger demanding the threads to lead me back

towards the lines on his hands before they lost their heat.

There's a door, another door beyond that to the outside —
we are trapped in *neither here nor there* where he is dead but not nearly buried

and we will have to answer questions correctly
to move to the next round, through a third and final door we have yet to notice.

Bonus points for remembering when my parents' young son was exhumed
and resituated, a conversation that almost plunders my mother of her last reserves,

she curls close to the polished table, a loose claim on my hand,
as her elder children outdo each other with feats of memory.

My mother focuses on the dresser.
Her breeding means she always has an eye for fine furnishing

and the room is a hurricane with the eye on the move,
was it ninety five or six, this overladen minutiae,

must the street we grew up on have a possessive case applied
when black and whited into the internet announcements,

and other cash-up-front social oracles announcing arrangements
we'd give anything to not have arranged,

seven local radio plays to get the word out,
a whirl in the parish notes for the masses,

until we are silenced,
assured that there won't be a sinner in the town

unaware of what this day has taken.

Inarticulate

Grief seals me airtight, brass screws tighten my extremities.
I'm told that settling earth takes time.

> Two months travelled
> *sorry for your loss*

and if my kitchen sparkles, clothes fester in a bedroom corner.
If I spend all my small talk,
> *a happy day for the man*
> there's nothing left to clot the silence.

> We offered tokens to his keeping,
slid between the coffin's tweed lining and the fabric of his suit jacket —
> *he went easy in the end*
screwdrivers; a faze tester;
> a replica of a ring he made a grandson;
> my book that he was too drugged up to read;
a photo of his lost child (the son my mother swears came to shepherd him.
> *hurry up, James*, she said, *come on, boy*)

We perched his glasses on his nose. We touched his hair, his eyebrows.

> I stayed awake while he rested
> in the box in the living room.

We left the kettle unboiled. I ran Fr So-and-So
> when he came to fill our mouths with his Hail Glory Be's. I breakfasted
> on the look in his eyes,
> nearly kissed the priest's pursed lips.

*"I did not feel safe or unsafe, but somewhere in-between,
liminal, passing from one life to another"*

DEBORAH LEVY
from *The Cost of Living*

I Look for my Father, But I

1.

      can't go home, can't go to where heights and ages skittered into the living room doorframe. I tried, after my father died: the month's mind, the birthday weekend when she changed her age without him, gluts of time over Christmas.

      can't go there anymore because he won't be waiting. I've been to where he is, of course I have. I have been to his graveside, five times if you count the occasion I left the morning after the month's remembrance mass.

      drank too much, hidden in the downstairs spare room with the light off as sisters and nieces roamed outside the small hall. The tea and sandwiches and apple pie made me feel like he died all over again. The polystyrene cup and bottle of merlot kept the cold to itself.

      came to in my car, in a petrol station parked up by the low wall opposite the graveyard, focussing and unfocussing on the horizon to attempt to select his headstone from the sea of stone crosses, angels, flat marble obelisks. If the light hits the field of stone just right.

      can go west to east, chronological demises, divide it into maternal and paternal losses, try recall their voices, how their mouths would shape around the four syllables of a name I shed like old clothing a long time ago.

      see them all, in their own way, the man from my mother's side, how he'd arrive on a Sunday evening, settle in the smokey living room for an hour or two, if I shut my eyes I am a child again, warmed by their talk, the laughs wisping through the floorboards.

      have them all tucked carefully in the folds of my cerebral cortex, but don't touch, don't.

2.

There are traces of my father in this kitchen, from one of the days he arrived into the yard, his Landrover facing the road and him sat waiting for me to return from the office job I despised.

He'd do that: arrive, wait, stand taking in the garden before it was a garden, the house before it was the home where my wife when she was a wife and I would and would not raise our children.

He'd hit the road early, telling no one and he'd come, steady and real. He was good like that, my father. There are traces of him in this kitchen, when he came with only the clothes on his body and the money in his pocket, stayed for days, (there must have been a row) this kitchen sings of that time, the lightbulb over my head is latched into the fitting he installed.

Appliances run through eco-cycles on power from the outlets he devised; the worktop himself and one-time-some-time-my-wife went for — she had to reverse his trailer in the builders' yard and he was man enough to let her.

He was like that, proud of her years of doing the silage in the midlands. Tractors and rolling bails. "If you've any odd bits and pieces, I'll do them for you," he'd say. Toolbox already open, organised.

3.

Where am I again. He's dead isn't he, and the shelves in my daughter's room,
intended to hold powders, cloths of muslin, cotton, wipes and salves
above the old drawers we requisitioned as a changing table are emptying.
He's here in furnishings I lay hands on daily, but where is he, really?

In the ward of the living dead, time is borrowed, according to the symbol
adorning the nurses station. Triquetra *from the Latin triquetrus*
Trinity of affection, pilfered from pagans for the title pages of protestant bibles,
promise rings and other naïve and sentimental items, the vow is the thing,
   till death etc
symbol of the completion, the shrouds in the cupboard confirm this,
they'll remake the bed, present his body clean as a chasuble.

December(s)

2018

Interior: Day. Scene opens —

the kind-eyed doctor; his science
tells us both what is not working

2019

Interior: Night. Scene opens —

it's not me, it's medicine
it's not medicine, it's me

I recognise joints and tendons
sluggish, inflamed past the point of pain

I don't see that man anymore; have figured ways
of self-soothing my body that don't hang like a threat

Dr K, armed with C-Reactive Protein score
ponders stress, lifestyle, preoccupation

above my head, slowly dripping into me while all around
the dying are living, living and dying. I can tell one from the other
a curtain pulls around the treatment chair when
the news is bad. I watch their shuffling feet

Nothing else in my mind besides my father's face
after the fact, waxen, before the undertaker

these are the months
my death-do-us-part stumbles to a halt, dead
sentiment, do not resuscitate

but I will not learn that today
I will not write the way it fell asunder
there will be time enough, slow time, for all of that

My father is dirty water sluicing through my veins
the cold of Rath graveyard bothers me like an insult

I admit he has a fine view of the mountains
the way they push forward into the blue of the day
he'd appreciate the chatter of those walkers
who treat the route by him like a thoroughfare

How dark it is at night, careless dogs cross over him
dig up unsettled earth and weather-battered flowers
His name isn't yet carved on the headstone
Kindly Kneel and Pray

the stonemason did a fine job. tidy, precise chisel
a wealth of gravel, some blue stone, some white
first pictures came in the summertime, Dad's name abbreviated
his role shortened too, the way he liked it, T.o.m, D.a.d
enough to know it is really him

The kind-eyed doctor searches
for tissues, finds hand-towel grease paper. Instead, I blot
my glasses on my shirt, the same I wore when he died

weeks past the stonemason and his summertime enterprise
we're facing Christmas again and I drive my mother to his graveside
his wife, my mother in my passenger seat in her red slippers
the radio on as I dig the little flower bed with a spoon, then my hands
push cyclamen roots of Christmas whites and reds
to earth themselves like he did
I scrub the prayer stone with blue paper
I will learn days later that rain does not wash away the remains of jostled soil

My clothes are all the same, except for shoes, socks, underwear
I thought I'd burn the whole rigout but instead once or twice a week
I hurry them from wet to dry, reassert those shapes on my body

> *the threads give way months into this ritual*
> *Small holes, rendering into larger holes*
> *I laid the clothes to rest in a drawer*
> *beside small child vests*
> *little swimsuits, a sock*
> *souvenirs of motherhood I will not sacrifice*
> *despite the separation: marital*
> *biology's bloodless war*

to bring the last of him around with me. My father is in the neck of my shirt
I know it because I leaned over his right side and pressed my forehead
to where his heart should have been beating. I held his cooling hands in
mine

> *those nights 'after' when I rested by his head*
> *on the good chair pulled from the good table*
> *my arms at coffin height*
> *as close as we would ever be again*

The shoulder stitching carries the handprint
of the pastoral worker whose face I never saw

> *the hospital staff read prayers at the All Souls' Mass*
> *the grieving were offered souvenir candles*
> *his name was under August on a poster on a plinth*
> *they read out his name, placed alphabetically with Q*
> *some died before him, some after, but you'd never know it*
> *I huddled back in the arch outside*
> *having legged it at the first lilt of Amazing Grace*
> *I watched a woman slap her small son*
> *as she hauled him back up the steps*

My head down on his chest, my eyes wetting his last clean pyjamas

my hand in his hair, on his arm, ulna and radius firm beneath his skin, his suit jacket

the worker's hand heavy with kindness while S or M told her I *had just arrived*
I am *his youngest* and I know I thought of Heaney, the neighbours and
   Big Jim Evans

I kept the first white feather safe in Heaney's 100 Poems

I remember wanting to shrug her off but that would have transformed the room
My father was never rude, preferring to warm-chat strangers out the door
the way he did with the priest when he came with his oils, his soft talk, so

days and nights in, he and I are
company kept by widow-screams I will always wish I never heard

I let that woman perform her ritual, later, I let him
alone when the young nurses came
to clean my father, pack the green and purple hospice bag
so full of his belongings that I snapped the strap while waiting
for the lift with M
and her arms full of his pillows, his phone charger
the precise/exact/all or nothing underpants I bought with Clodagh out in Wilton
(or was it Douglas), the pyjamas it took three of us to cut the legs and
   sleeves off
for his drips, drain bags, monitors

they too are in fragments safe in my keeping
swatches of blue check pyjamas
the last to touch his living body

we tried so hard to find the humour in it. Those girl nurses must
have removed his drain his port, all the plasters and dressings. I know they
   washed him with a flannel
trimmed a lock of his hair for my mother, she has it in her handbag last I heard

take from my memory, the loss of him, the way it severed her
she quakes like a war cry, is ravaged like the dead-in-waiting

ii

So, I suppose this is a remaking
And we must be remade.

I'm filling shelves with books I forgot to read years ago,
making banana bread fortnightly but must always look up
ingredients, improvise measurements

> *cookies I accept I do not accept I thought*
> *you were making banana bread. A joke*
> *he would have made.*

No, not now. I'm filling my ears
    with Carrie & Lowell
illumination illumination wood blocks hiss in the grate

I've the window open to catch tyre gauges on the baile, idle my
brain, identify neighbours, hum of the fast fella in the red van
the trundle of the inefficient farmer, men who look at us in suspicion

till they discover that the woman I married is fluent

> *in words from someone else's mouth*

in agriculture

and I'm competent at mechanics

> *I rebuild, meticulous, logically*

cars, the abiding principles of electricity

We're making a home here at last, chest of drawers by storage unit

I tried for my babies, I tried
stayed longer than I should have

My mother says grey is no colour
but I'm wearing it under purple today so I guess that's alright

blackonblackonblack

The blueberries mould-melted but I dug last summer's strawberries
from the ice, pushed them into the bread batter with the flat of my knife

I no longer bake in the afternoons, no small hands
in mine beyond the designated Saturdays, sometimes Sundays

I fill my hands rather than remember how he held them to his mouth
let loose the contents of a putrid stomach

J and I stood outside the door as they cleaned him up
we will never speak about it to each other

I now own fingerless Aran-knit gloves, they'll warm my palms
inside and out, keep his last touch in the etchings no matter what
    plates I have spinning
There's a question no one can answer and it is *where does the love go*

stays in the crick of your neck

I am doing all the right things. I call my mother; buy Poinsettias
    for the fireplace
like she used to, joke about attacks — asthma vs panic and which
    one will/will not kill you
and on we go

are/am you/I dead yet?

It is a remaking, we must be remade, trust the trusting, trust he left
    us enough
of himself in our marrow to get us by and we can wire in cookers
    by phone-light

know I can start again
brave new love and its soft promises

sell cars at a profit, plan plastering jobs, build flatpack furniture and
    fill shelves
with all our forgotten volumes, and in the process of remembering
we will remake ourselves

*"Many people live and die without ever
confronting themselves in the darkness"*

CARMEN MARIA MACHADO
from *Her Body and Other Parties*

Salthill, Friday morning

Jimmy makes the best lattes in Galway,
across from where the joggers stretch
and men halt brisk walks so their dogs
can defecate at leisure. Jimmy knows my order
by heart. I come early, as I did all that first summer
after the news that a threat loomed within my father.
Jimmy's latte cools on the dash, pencils and pen
in my hands, I'm parked up at the shoreside carpark
and ready to work. This day is everyday,
will be ever the same, no matter who or what
the ground elsewhere has swallowed.

Devotion

After Patti Smith

She asks me to pour her wine before she leaves
the house, and I do it, pour myself a draft as well
in an unclean bulb, tainting an otherwise fresh pour.

Isn't it just like me to turn this into more
than I deserve. The fire is out. We make things.
She does her utmost to unmake them,

a far more severe endeavour than "to break".
To hand I have this pencil, her favourite
density for shading. I have Patti Smith and her slick tokens.

Her way with time — Patti Smith's, that is — to her, loving
is the same as remembering, as keeping company.
The poet told me once that there are no wrong words.

I need to pencil in an hour to tell her I found them
on the tip of my tongue. The person I married
found her words behind someone else's teeth.

Shannagurraun, near the end

Enough bogland and rush thicket to keep
the happiest of truffle pigs in muck.
Enjoy your time with the children,
they warn how I stand to lose
the words I've worked so hard to win.
If "momma" never reaches my ears again,
cut down in a throat's memory,
I'll remember how we chose those
cherry blossoms, one pink, one red,
promised them to the earth,
and this is where those words will stay,
each shovel of soil, every dust of rooting powder
an encouragement. Our daughter huddled
into the crouch of my body. We made
a triptych of barely grown things
for you to capture and discard,
bird wing, scapula, don't press too hard
for too long. All things will find a place to break.

Lost/Losing [Teeth, part 2]

Miles west of me, a first loss keeps under a small girl's pillow
chin-dropped voice-secrets "Momma, I miss you, my tooth falled out"
My opposite considers naught missed, a woman surely set to ruin me
make mincemeat of my breathing and how it all went to hell at her hand

To eradicate (read: remove) X, focus isotopes like a knife to all
the promises ever spoken to a body in the dead black
To eradicate (read: displace), Z, target all cells that need a going over
Arrah, if the light is hazed, just shoot the lot, we haven't the time

The delicate soldiers of healing part to let the priest waltz in
With his vaudeville patter, all robes and flourish, damp palms
To remove (read: relegate) tension, thrum between shoulder blades
Choose gouging point, mark it with a letter you will never speak again

Abscond

Verb

        to leave hurriedly   secretly

           Biological
                  Maternal
                      Mother

These are the days
           of the wild verbs

                        of non-

                            connective tissue

How To Unmake

1. Delicately prise child arms from around one mother's neck
(You will need to do this at least twice)
2. Do not accept the recalcitrance of clasped fingers
small foreheads in a neck's crook
3. You may have to tackle small, interlocking
ankles but be direct. Begin at hip, femur
4. Protect yourself from the harshness
of patella against mandible. Little legs
are stronger than they seem
5. Remember, those long commands
of fibula and tibia gained their stature
alongside-trailing-behind-in-the-arms-of the woman
whose services you no longer require
6. Once liberated, use both hands
to gather child fragments, small painted toenails
summer-damp knees, little questioning mouths
7. You need to unsee any tears, for this, comfort yourself
with the benign placation of another's body in your bed
8. Tell yourself just how happy you really are

What would Tom Quirke say

What would he make of this brick by brick dismantling
of a life so meticulously crafted. I learned the weight
of words from him, how to hold the consonants
of matrimony in my mouth. I learned from him
the best days of company: how to love my family
like a glove loves a hand, with the same ease a bed
cradles a sleeping body. To miss him is to recognise
my body without blood. He is the hardest loss to reckon,
more than skin, bone, her. How would he view
the alterations of a house unbuilt, the way I must learn
to mother my children from a distance.

Cento from Journal

The fertility clinic sent a letter,

Hungover. Undercooked eggs.
All the Saturdays I didn't join her
In the kitchen.
                              Epiphany is
A dinner party where the most important
Person is the one who is not
At the table.
                              Shakespeare
And a Divided America.

Someone I no longer recognise
Consuming something I can't stomach.

She doesn't answer my calls anymore.
It's like she has taken on all our failures
And her body can't hold it in.

Juno and Nova were happy,
Late morning in pajamas.

I am worried about Juno.

Juno and Nova had a movie day.

I drove to Armagh with Kae Tempest
In my ears.

                    I couldn't tell her why
I loved her,
                    what I remembered.

Anything.

                    Everything.

The couch and armchairs.

Geese

Only ribcages
when she found them
picked sky clean
apart from wings
whole, outstretched
awaiting flight.

Ways I heal myself

She has me to hold, for now, if she wants me.
        I give her this moment of my keeping.
It's too easy to offer all I am away to others.
        Their strange bodies make me tired.
My cells draw in just enough earthly elements
        to raise my chest slowly,
once then twice, smooth and deep, enough space
        for a voice to break in the small hours.
I'm waiting for when she turns me back
        to tide-height, an apology from her lips.

I'll stand it well — take the message into my legs
        and walk it back to the earth.
She is kind enough to let me rest for a while
        in the possibility of her,
of more than we are apart,
        before she opens her hands and away I go,
divided into the mouths of strangers
        who reward my recklessness with bruises,
their honest, brutal kisses. I won't forget
        hands I've invited onto my body.

I won't forget how I instructed them
        to claim my skin, unknowingly,
the way a stranger's tongue in my mouth
        is only incomprehensible the first time.
How I keep the firmness of his arms,
        the cool of her teeth as artefacts
to archive the ways I chose to cure myself.
        And I remember everything,
except their names, everything
        except the colour of their eyes.

Thinking of you, I have noticed the following....

The cold isn't as sharp, since that first pint
in Neachtain's doorside snug
where on arrival, you mapped the whole interior,
panel after wood panel
and facing your concealed commotion,
I surveyed how your quiet nerves rattled.

Still as tomorrow, I watched you clock
every ragged poster
and each ancient lampshade in the place,
a lunch menu we were too early for,
back to the table top again until finally,
you laid blazing eyes on me.

How was I to predict
beyond that first kiss in Garavan's
that I'd end up carrying your pulse
to my mask-drop seascapes
where I let questions tear at my skin
like riptides and all the air is threat
and squander, contortions
that can't compete
with the way you hold me in my rest.

Expected but never. This.
Us together and this day's light
asks if until now a living skin
had been mine to claim.
But it doesn't matter how
or why you came,
I'm years from my Prom-side
Winnebago mystics,
instead I'll count my own cards
to see if I can get this one hand right.

All I know is I'll weather miles
to feel the way you flood
my blood with life.
Because of you,
my eyeline has a new horizon
and I think of you beyond my line of sight,
a few hours east of where I stand
and you should know,
even when I'm far from you,
my eyes held
by the rigging of a sleeping crane,
my thoughts on this Tuesday of our first November
are of you, of you, only you.

Sacrificial Wind

for Lorna Shaughnessy

A night of quiet company, the Town Hall's Studio still
but for the unconscious breaths of strangers
waiting for your Agamemnon to speak his great regret.

Thigh to thigh we cluster in the cheap seats,
and I with no mind yet to touch the Greeks,
invite your lines to blaze ancient worlds to life

with enough flame to sear the cost of sacrifice, Euripides' lesson
a humming scar on malleable tissue, muscle, heart, memory.
Now our years have laid themselves to rest

and the current swell has gifted us more loss than can be borne.
And what of your Aulis now? What of those left behind
now we know the heavy labour of burying our remembered dead?

Lorna, these are the losings we teach each other — our parents lost
and leaving — acts that you in your quiet way cannot rewrite.
And know I'd rather meet you anywhere but these high winds

Iphigenia was sacrificed to swell. But we are two women–children
mourning the men we've buried, our losses in shards mosaic-small,
dust in winds that decide who shall leave and who shall stay behind.

Everyday's A Good Day Now

Under my window, a fella lumbers spent wheelie bins up a stocky flight of redbrick. It's a dry day in September and all of us are alive. Under my window, the aul boys absolve each other of the day's mild sinning. Is there anything more ordinary than two men crossing ways with nothing rattling around in their heads and the world confined to the few steps ahead of them? The steady seal of the front door at their closing, then dinner across the table from their wives, perhaps a late phonecall from a daughter. And what's left of the promise of his last good days, my father in his stand-up hope, shuffling across the hospital atrium, his drips and drain bags, slow wheels and an upright pole to keep him steady, a metal cane one day, a metal frame another, the way he bestowed the gifts of his favour on a woman whose husband would leave that space under his own steam. Hope is a dying man wishing a healed man good health. Their goodbye a quick cortege ahead of its time. And what's worse? To shake hands with strangers till all strength leaves a body or to resign forever to greet men with no complaints: "Sure, everyday's a good day now."

Love letter to my father

Dad, I've been talking to the dead,
but no word yet. Just a scything wind
to clip the legs right off me.

I leave gifts at times, where we've masoned your name
to see if any claw lays claim, rummage for telltale
turnings in the gravel. Down by the graveyard

wall last night, I muddled ways to count your absence.
(The sum of days to night are easy.
Occasions, cakes and candles, easy too.)

When it's dark at the boundary between
the living and the rest, I see footholds where
pointing fell to dust, witness spectral scrambles up

and over, your horseshoes lurking full of luck,
ghosts of matchboxes snicked by rifle-shot pellets,
the duppy of your brother's once-kept horses.

They trample buds and snuffle ghostly feedbags.
These freezing nights, heat lifts off their long-dead bodies
hulking reminders of what looms in the dark.

In my nightly haunting, I gut myself like a fish
to lay it all out before you. Your wife is as she will be.
There's a hole though, she's shot through spine to sternum

from lack of you. The nights thin the barrier between
ye and I listen to her calling in the chill. You both
modelled this way of living. Taught me in the ways you

held each other. My first teachers, and my absent advisor,
can you see me? Can you see all I try to do to pay tribute
to you, to her, to all you left behind?

Madame Helena on the Prom

A move, a change and a challenge,
says Helena over crystals after I've parted with my cash.

At Salthill Prom at mid-tide on a sunblushed Tuesday,
I spot her tacking a day-glo poster on the windscreen,
she calls to me, a siren song in plush velvet,
Let Madame Helena tell you your future.

I count my steps back to the Avensis,
pledge to whatever power I am now praying,
if I've cash in the car, I'll go back, what harm?

Tell your mother not to worry, she says, not specifically, like,
but in synonym, the way she smacks my hand, sucks her teeth.

Helena has a booster pack for the mobile phone
that could carry her voice all the way to the sky above,
but she's soft with me, *It won't always be like this*, she promises.

like she can see my wedding ring moved from finger
to car-dash ashtray. *A move, a change and a challenge,*
she says, after I've parted with my cash.

I was young. (I'm still young) I will have *no more children.*
The two I have were *born lucky, not rich,*
lucky, not rich (She says this twice, no flies on Helena.)
High honours, a settled bed by the water
and there I will find peace (and there I will find peace).
Her hand on mine around the crystal which keeps
my money where her mouth is; *no more pain*, she says,
no death and I ask her if sense can come from nonsense.

Good news will come in the post. Good news will spill in the waves.
She says I am strong and I will rise (I nearly believe her)
to a height that will surprise friends and family.
(I say feck anyone who is surprised)

The good friends I have around me, I'll keep.
She sees regret *across the aisle* but the days of that love
are past. My daughters *will wear uniforms*, my eldest girl,
will she truly be a nurse, or is the youngest off to Templemore?

Will I pass them all I have like a draw rope,
latch, pulley, lever, strength, discipline.
And I'll *be happy*, she says. An abstract notion —
mid-half-disaster, no matter how the sun shines in Salthill.

And I know Happy. It's books, my daughters.
Happy is tea shared with my father the last time
I saw him living. Helena wants to know my questions
and all my mind can utter: "What's next? Is it her? Is it her?

Is it her?" *Be brave*, says Helena, she says, *be brave, sure what
    have you* (left) *to lose.*

LIZ QUIRKE is a writer and scholar from Co. Kerry. Salmon Poetry published her debut collection *The Road, Slowly* in 2018. She teaches on the MA in Writing at NUI Galway and is completing a practise-based PhD on Queer Kinship in Contemporary Poetry.

salmonpoetry

Cliffs of Moher, County Clare, Ireland

"Like the sea-run Steelhead salmon that thrashes upstream to its spawning ground, then instead of dying, returns to the sea—Salmon Poetry Press brings precious cargo to both Ireland and America in the poetry it publishes, then carries that select work to its readership against incalculable odds."

TESS GALLAGHER

The Salmon Bookshop
& Literary Centre

Ennistymon, County Clare, Ireland

"Another wonderful Clare outlet."
The Irish Times, 35 Best Independent Bookshops